AF482153

CHRISTMAS PAPER CRAFTING
with Reny

BY RENATA KOLIBOVA

DEDICATION

TO MY WONDERFUL FANS ALL AROUND THE WORLD.

THANK YOU.

Foreword

I invite you to discover and enjoy the colorful world of paper crafts.

My second book will set you up for Christmas with 30 beautiful paper crafts with super clear-illustrated instructions.

I'm combining my years of experience as a kindergarten teacher and over 1000 crafts I've shared online, to convince you that crafting is really easy and fun to do!

When you finish this book you'll not only have created a beautiful home or school decorations but also lovely gift cards for holidays. I am sure you will enjoy them with your loved ones.

Merry Christmas!

Who's Reny?

I'm a kindergarten teacher and have been a craft blogger since 2015, making paper craft videos and tutorials.

I'm followed by millions of teachers and parents just like yourself from all around the globe.

Social Media

Find over 1,000 crafts on my social media blogs.

From fun animals and stunning gift cards to seasonal crafts to get you inspired all year long.

I'm busy crafting new ideas nearly every day, so you'll never run out of things to do.

Check me out at:

facebook.com/papermagicreny
youtube.com/papermagicreny
instagram.com/paper_magic_reny

It'd mean the world to me, if you shared pictures of your crafts with me.
Reach out on my Facebook or Instagram :)

Tips & Tricks

Here are quick instructions to make funny eyes and paper hooks.

The next pages will cover shapes and dimensions for all the crafts.

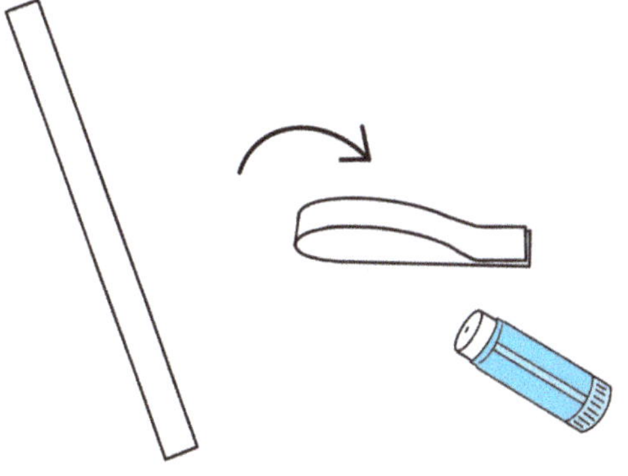

Tips for making circles

210 × 297 mm

**Any sheet
thickness**

Or

8.5 × 11 in

**Any sheet
thickness**

200 × 200 mm

8 × 8 inch

65 × 65 mm

2.5 × 2.5 inch

Tips for making strips

A4

210 × 297 mm

Any sheet thickness

Or

Letter

8.5 × 11 in

Any sheet thickness

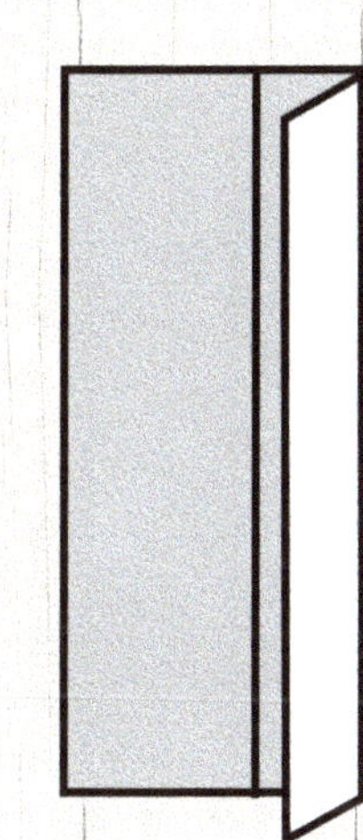

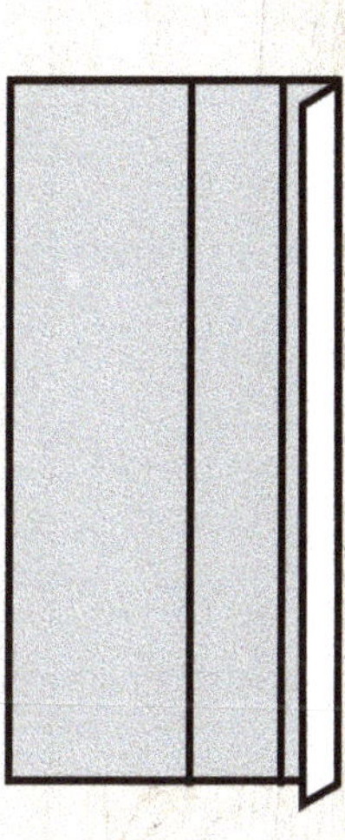

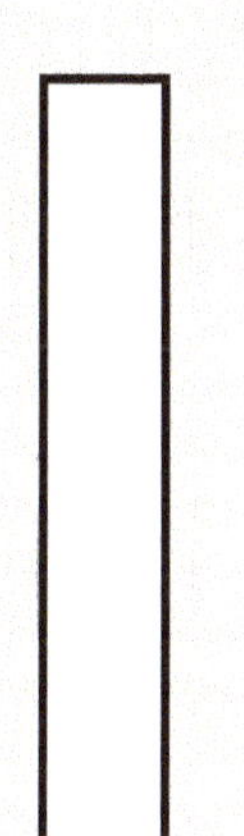

**1/2 of
A4 or Letter**

**1/4 of
A4 or Letter**

**1/8 of
A4 or Letter**

CHRISTMAS DECORATIONS

Crafts

Stocking

Christmas tree

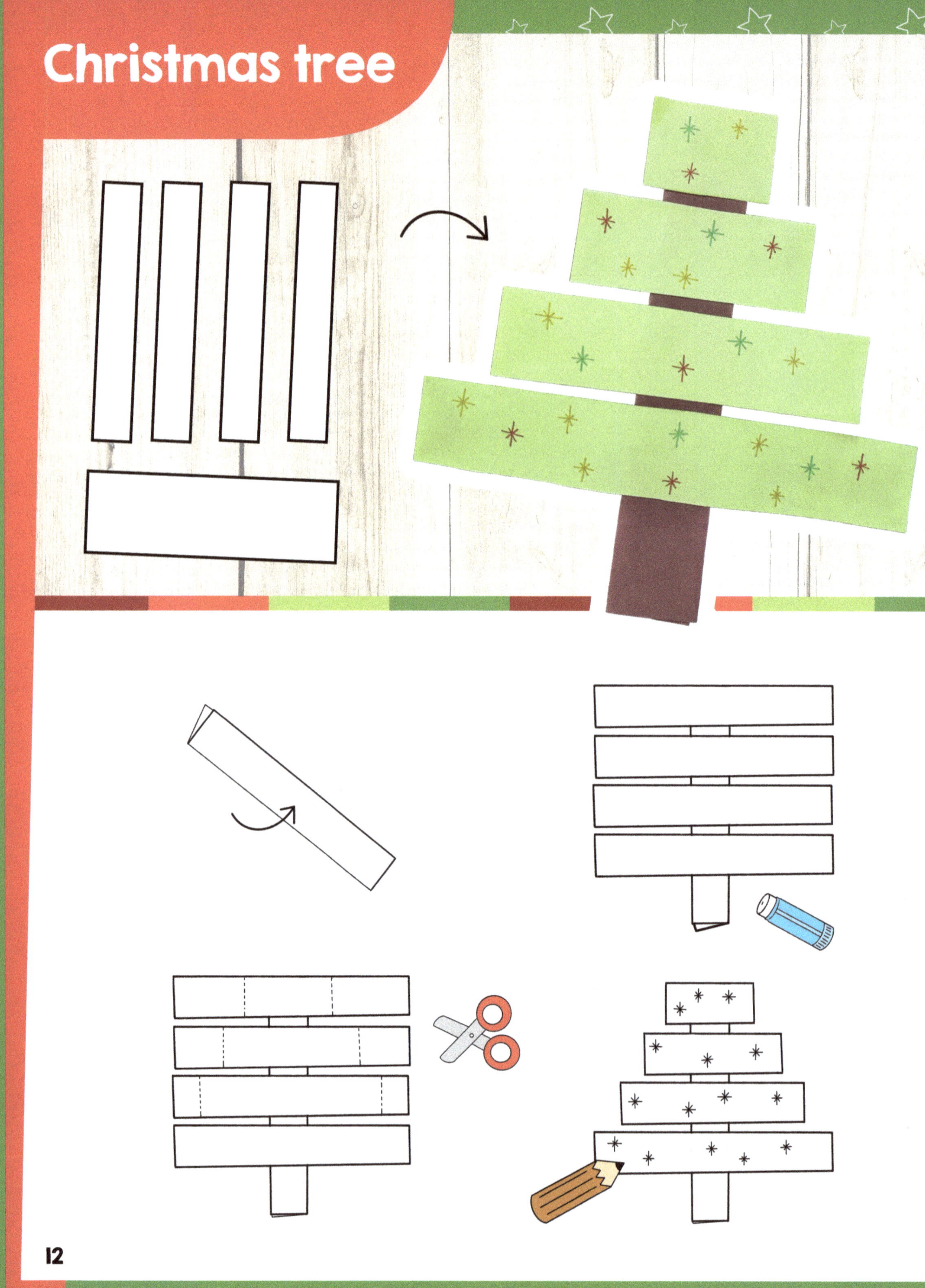

Candle

Wreath

Snowman

Christmas Star

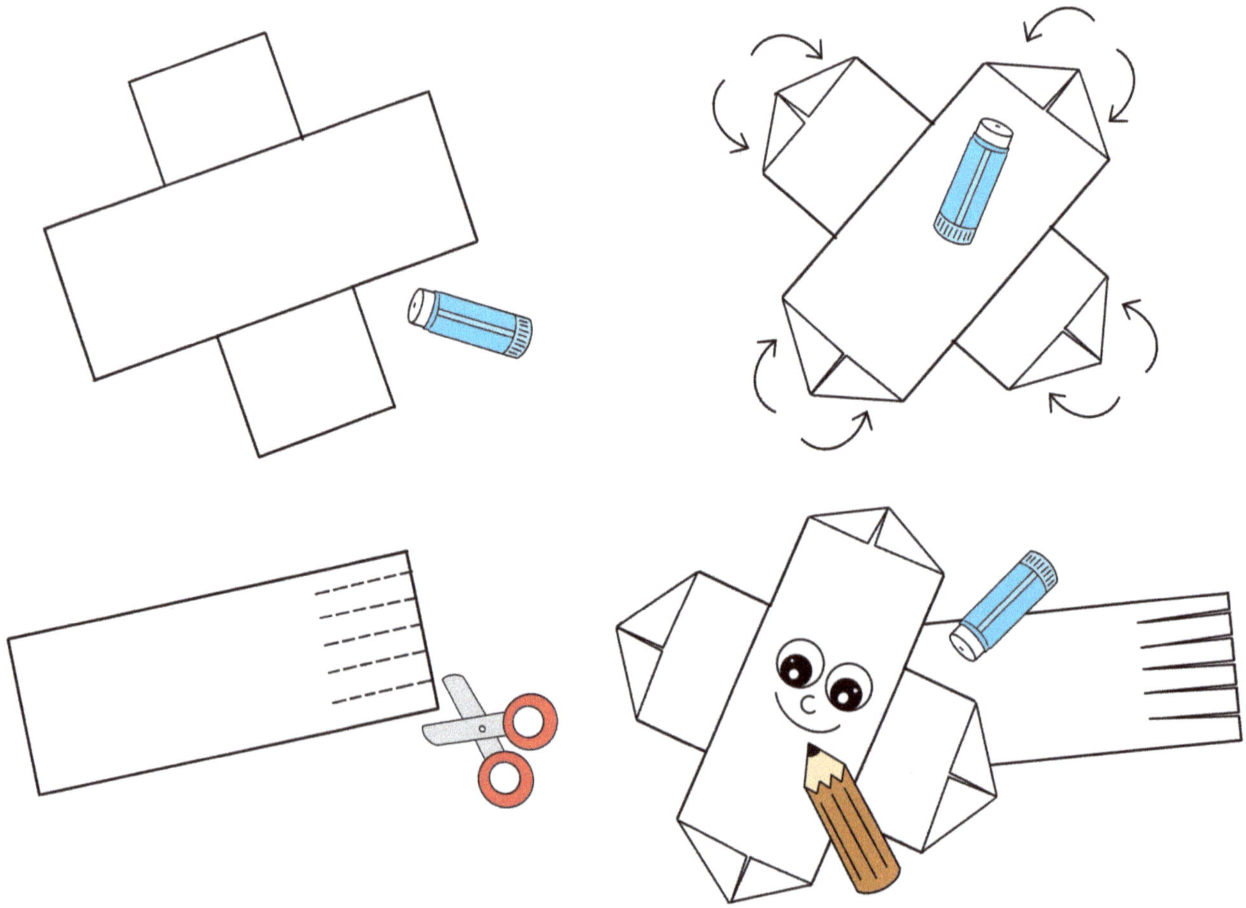

Christmas tree

Bell

Snowman

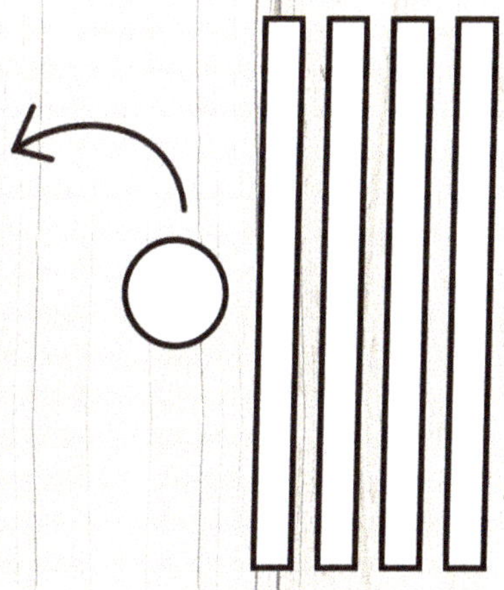

CHRISTMAS CHARACTERS

Crafts

Santa Claus

Rudolph

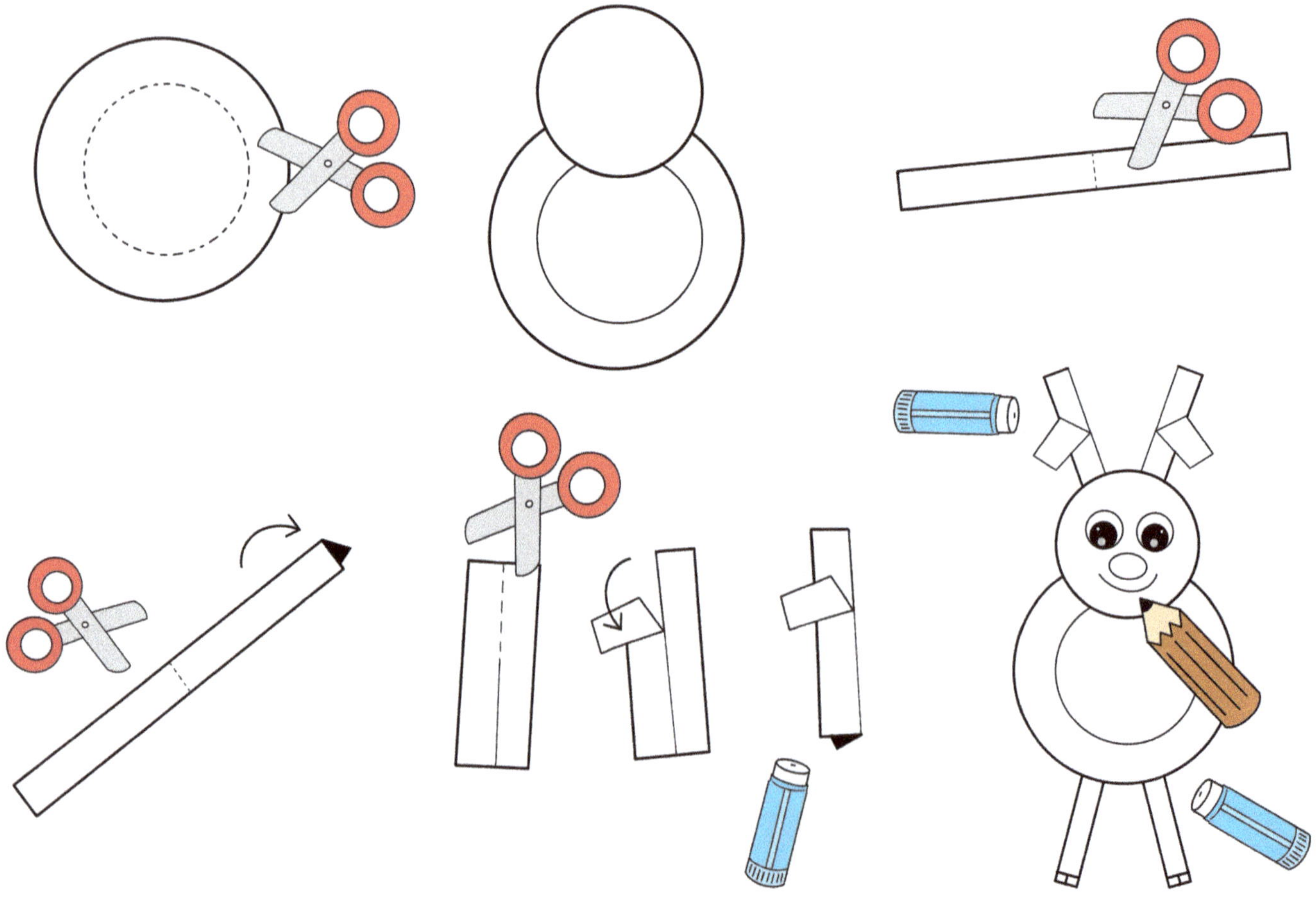

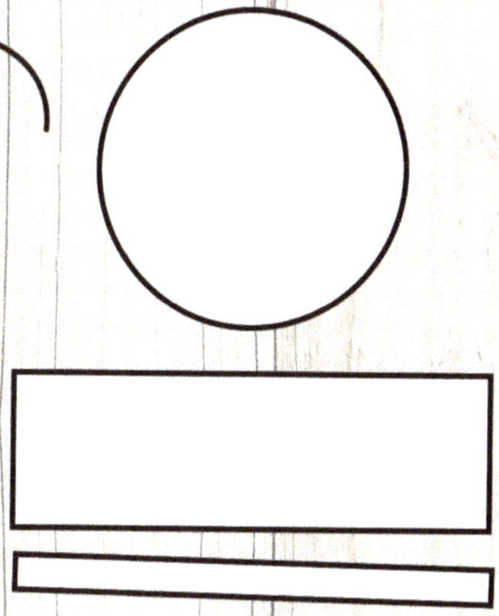

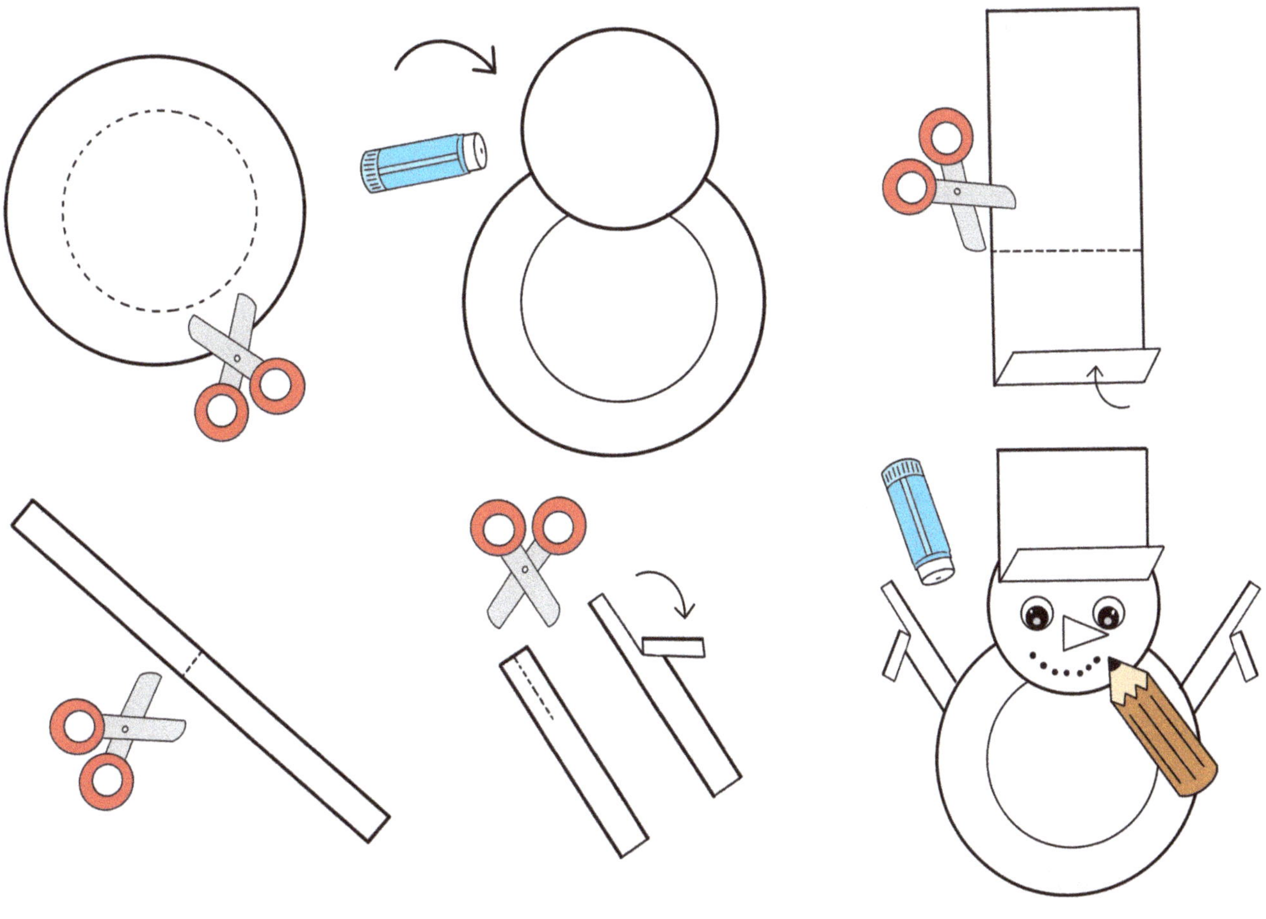

Elf

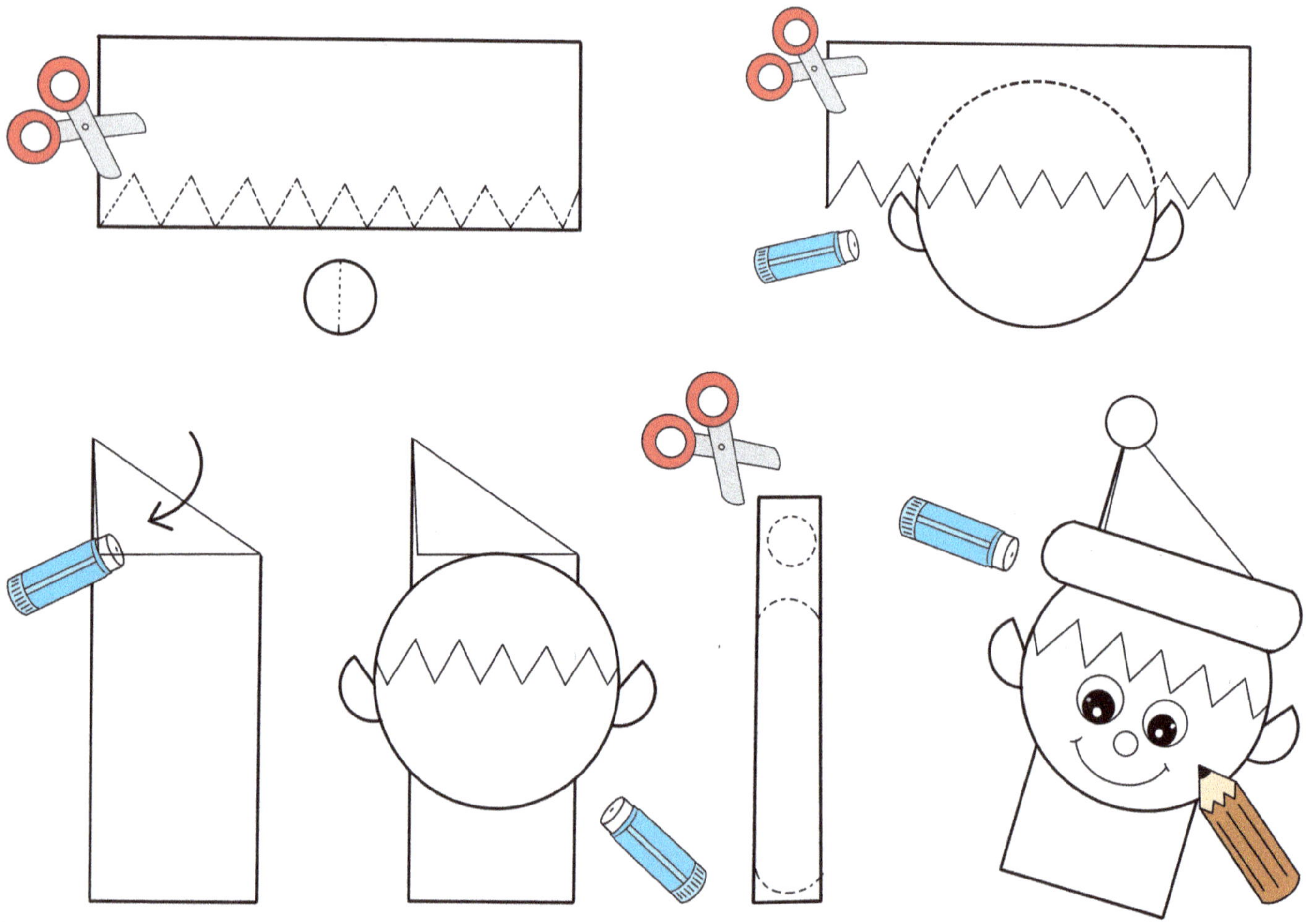

Angel

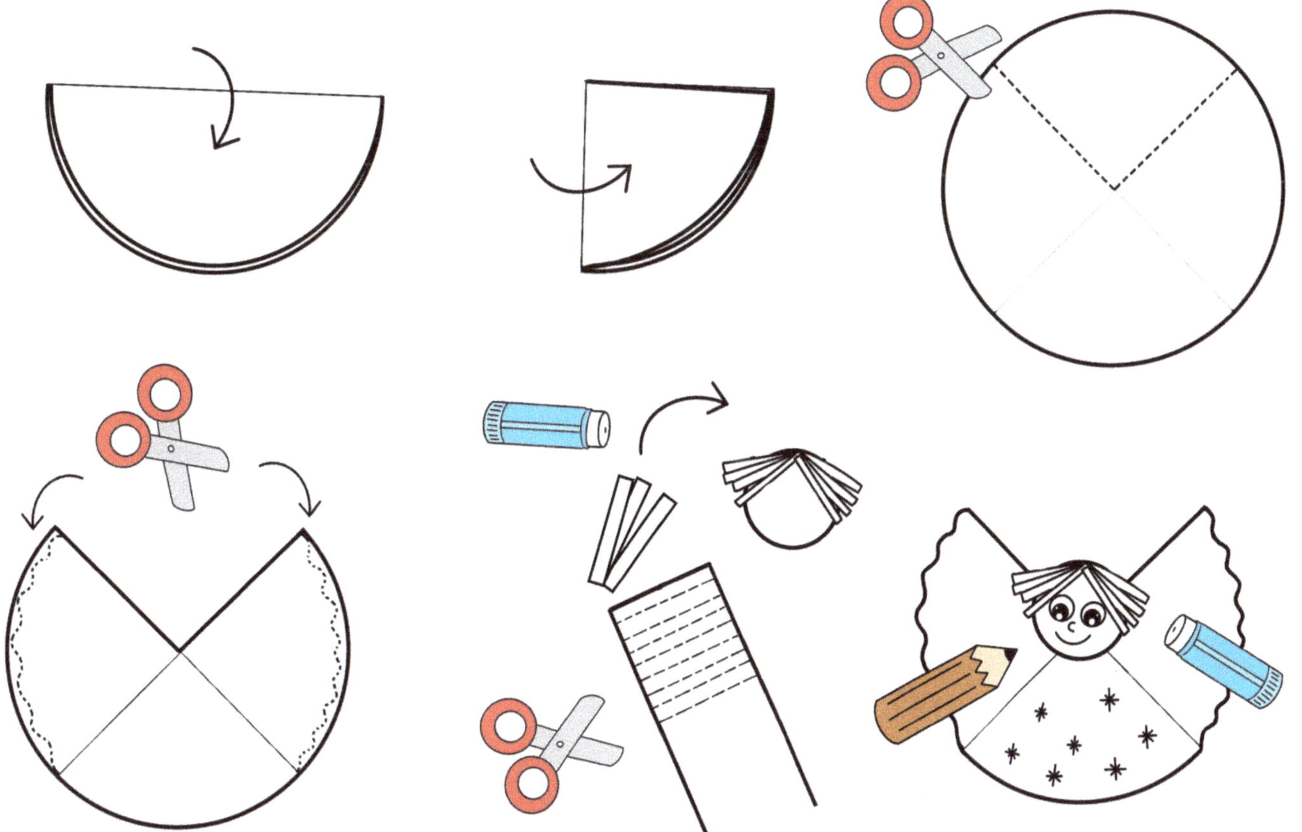

Snowman band

CHRISTMAS CARDS

Crafts

Angel

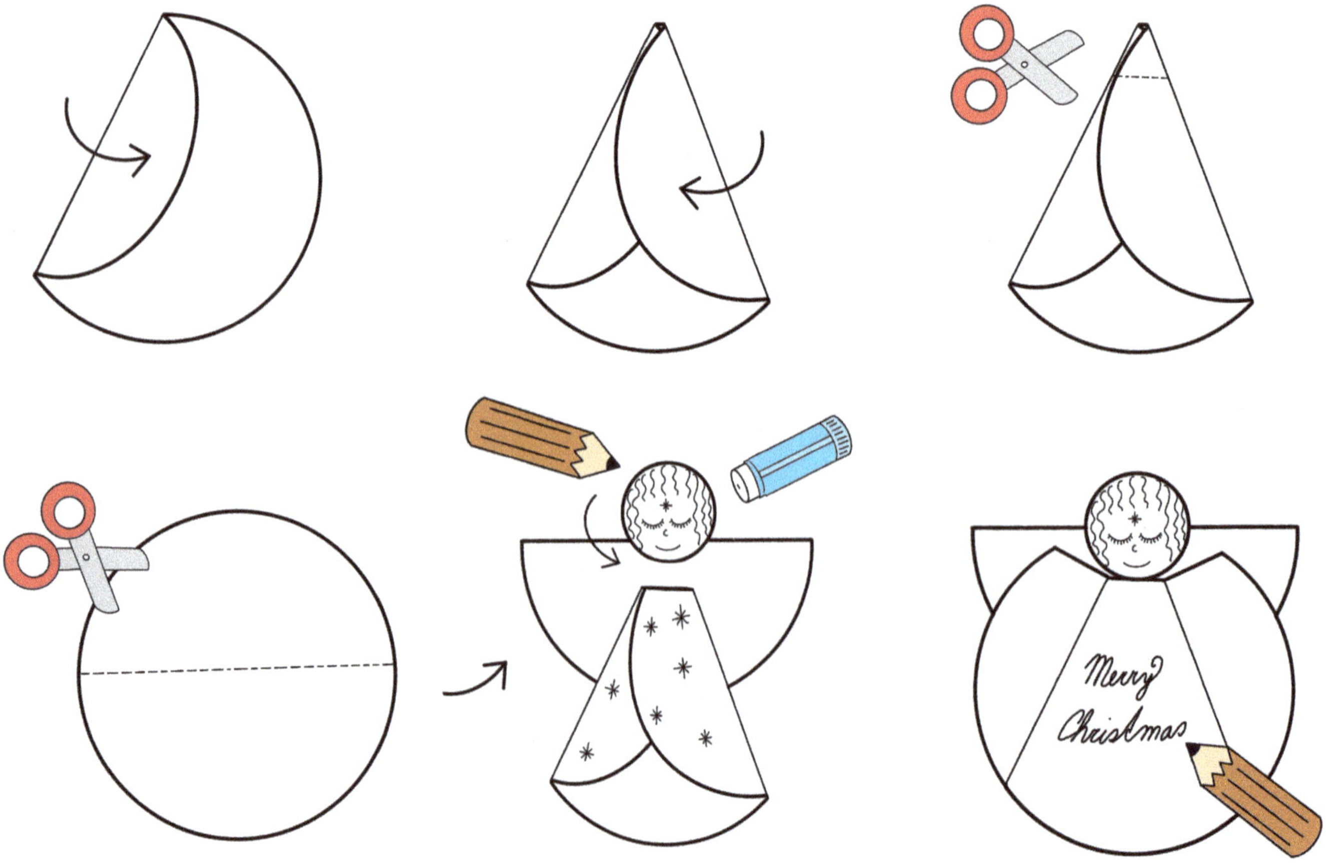

Bell

Snowman

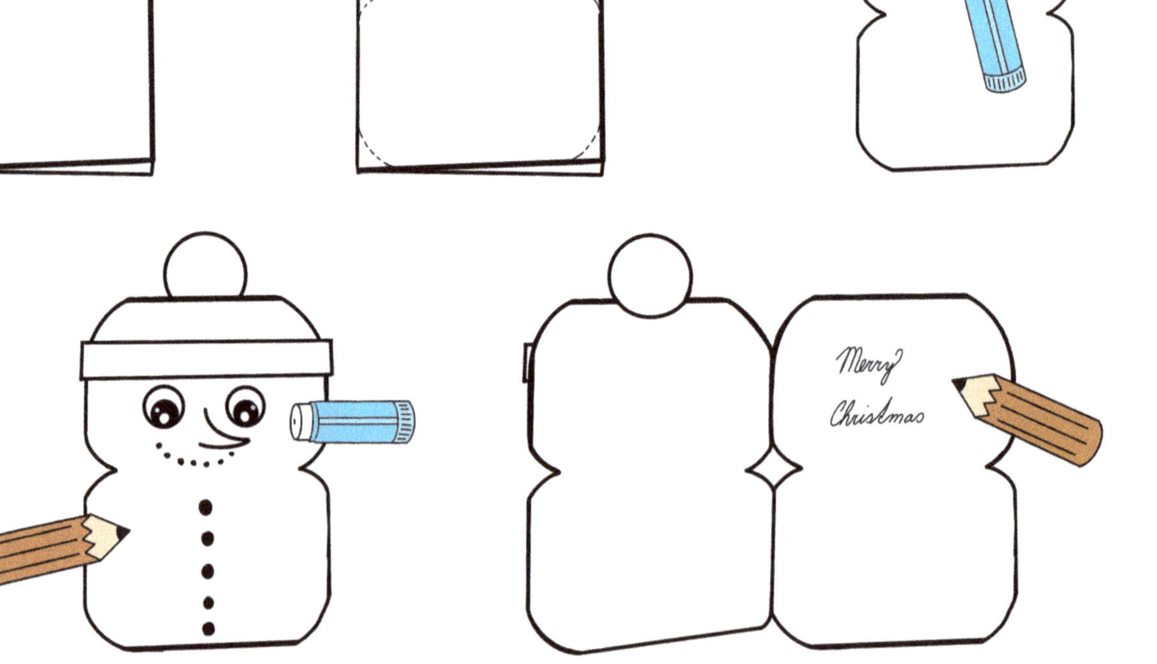

Merry
Christmas

Christmas ball

Merry Christmas

Christmas tree

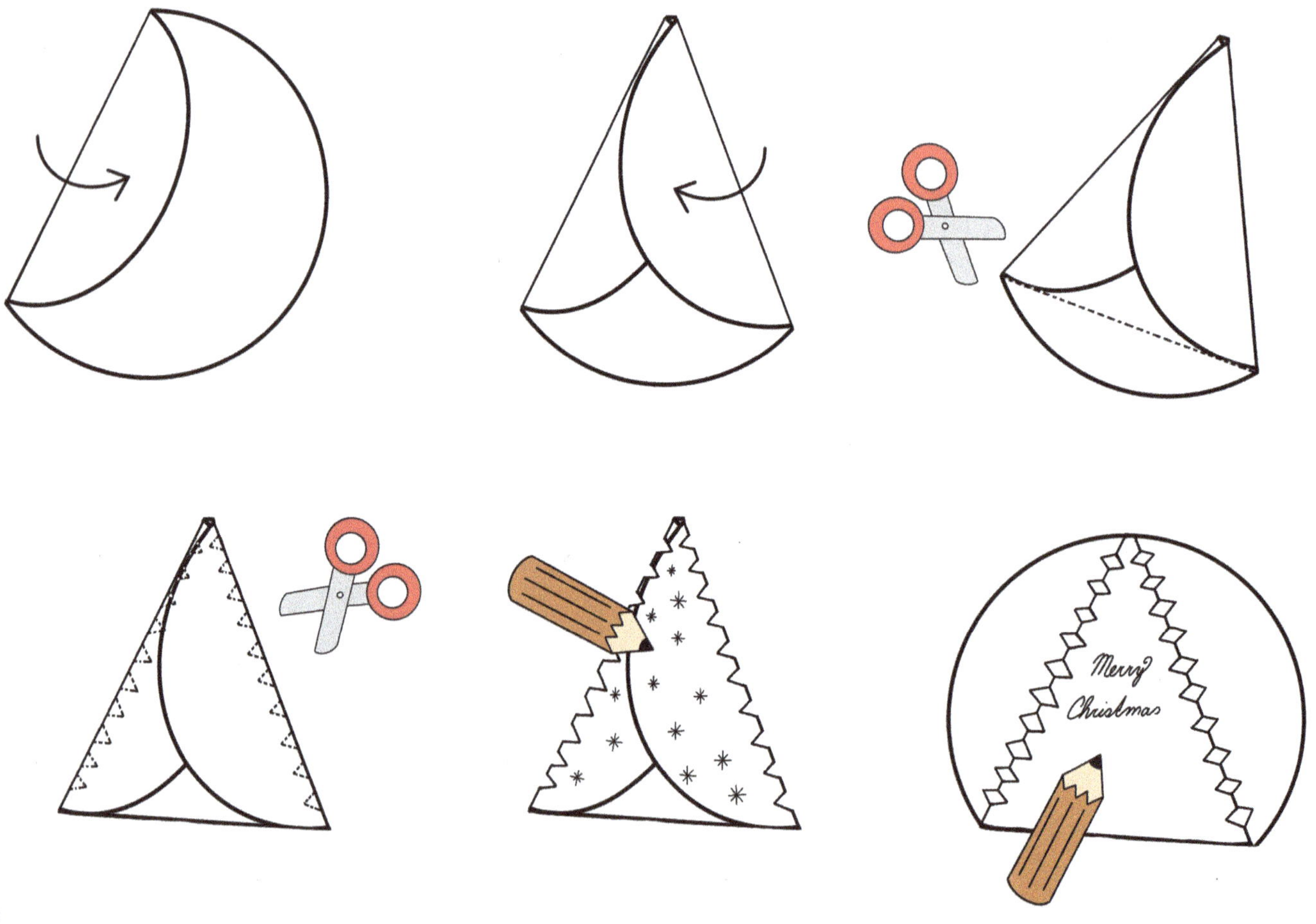

Penguin

www.ingramcontent.com/pod-product-compliance
Lightning Source LLC
Chambersburg PA
CBHW041819110726
48006CB00019B/2437